REASON, FAITH

&

EXPERIENCE

An Introduction to 21st century Quakerism

by Richard Hilken

First published in September 2006
Second Edition 2007
by
Exeter Fairway Publications
on behalf of Exeter Quaker Meeting

ISBN 1 871839 21.1
Copies obtainable from the Publishers
at
Exeter Fairway Publications
3 Patricia Close,
Exeter EX4 4RT

INDEX

Notes: *I have used the words "Friend" or "Quaker" interchangeably for individual members and the words "Quakers/ism" or "the Society" for the organisation.*

Where quotations are referenced, numbers such as '26.61' refer to Quaker Faith & Practice, 1994 edition..

Introduction

Quakers are seekers who do not believe that words can ever be an adequate means of defining spiritual matters and who try instead to seek the "Inner Light" through silent worship. We believe this Light can enlighten everyone in the world and has indeed done so since the beginning of time. Most Quakers prefer to speak of "the Light" or "Spirit", rather than "God", since this is how we experience the divine, as a guide or illumination of our way. This Light can be found in all people "where the heart stands in perfect sincerity".

I suppose I became a Quaker when I was about 15, although I did not realise it at the time. I loved the music of the Book of Common Prayer, but as I was taught more about Anglicanism, I came to realise that most of the things I was expected to believe seemed either unnecessary, like the virgin birth, or improbable, or even inconsistent with Jesus' teaching of a loving God such as the sacrifice of Jesus for the past sins of the world. I hoped that I would one day understand and accept these matters but, as the years went by, I found I was actually saying less and less of the Creed, finally only the first four words: "I believe in God", which nebulous phrase contained all of which I felt certain . My approach to religion had a huge boost at University, when the four Anglican Professors of Divinity held public lectures at which they in turn spoke of their own moral, historical, psychological and intellectual "Objections to Christian Belief". I was heartened by these lectures and the discussions which they engendered, and decided to persist with my membership.

Six years later however, one Sunday morning, our small daughter dragged me to the local Friends Meeting House to show me where her playgroup was held. We arrived just before Meeting and, noting my interest, a local Friend told me that they were having an outside speaker that evening and added that if I attended, no-one would subsequently follow me up. That last was crucial. I would never have gone if I had thought I might be doorstepped by religious weirdos. However, what the speaker said about the Inner Light showed me that my problems with doctrine were irrelevant. I realised that I had been a Quaker in all but name from my teens and from that evening I have never wanted to worship anywhere else.

I also learnt that day that Quakerism is far from being the gloomy Puritan sect many people imagine. Quakers recognise that the Spirit / Light can illuminate and inspire in ways beyond mere words, indeed words cannot ever adequately embrace the spiritual - as the Catholics have long known. But it is not only beauty that inspires, it is friendship, love - indeed all our experience, not forgetting humour, can be used to illuminate our spiritual life if we so choose. We have chosen a broad path and there is room for all on it.

This booklet is an attempt to give a picture of Quakerism which speaks not only to the many who have no Christian or other religious roots but also to those "believers" who have problems with doctrine. It attempts to answer questions about Quakerism by showing how our lives are grounded in our understanding of this Light and practised in our worship, in our lives and in the organisation of the Society. I hope it shows also that Quakerism is a joyful approach to religion, not the dour, negative one that its public reputation implies.

WORSHIP

The Centre

The focus of our corporate life is the Meeting for Worship, where we meet in silence and quietly wait on the Spirit. "Worship is our response to an awareness of God. .... In worship we enter with reverence into communion with God and respond to the promptings of the Holy Spirit." (1.02.8&9). A commitment to regular attendance at our Meetings is the outward sign of Membership, rather than having a clearly defined belief in the presence of the Spirit. While we traditionally refer to this as the Spirit or Light of Christ, we do not wish to imply that we see Jesus as being personally present in our Meetings, but rather that we experience that same Spirit which has inspired countless people over the millennia and which many believe was most truly reflected in the life of Jesus. We believe that this Spirit speaks to us today and most certainly not only (or even always) to Quakers. The Light is in everyone, of any religion, age or gender, though not everyone always pays attention to it. It is universal and omnipresent. We believe that we can recognise the workings of this same Spirit in secular literature, in poetry, art and music and indeed also in some scientific writings.

In our Religious Society we try to have no leader other than this Spirit. This puts a great responsibility on us to speak in our Meetings only when we are sure that what we have to say is truly for the worshipping group and is not just a reflection of our own concerns. We believe, and indeed on occasion experience, that there is a power present which we can rarely find on our own. In a meeting which is so led, the sense of presence can be almost tangible. Our worship is communal and, though we individually often pray alone, we recognise solitary prayer as something essentially different from the Meeting for Worship, not unlike the difference between practising football skills on your own and playing in a team, though the Spirit may well reach you in both.

We have no appointed preacher or leader, not because we do not recognise the need for someone to play a leading role from time to time, but rather because we believe that this role is open to all of us, minute by minute, as the Spirit may lead us. We therefore see ourselves as a "priesthood of all believers".

Anyone may speak in our Meetings, though we hope the ministry (we refer to spoken contributions as "ministry") will enhance the worship rather than disrupt it. We believe that we should resist the temptation to speak at length and only speak at all when we are sure that the time and the promptings in our hearts are right. This requires a discipline which we have developed over the years and whose guidelines are set out in our Advices & Queries 8, 9 & 10 (Chapter 1 of "Quaker Faith and Practice") which we try to follow faithfully. The words "advice" and "query" are also significant. We do not instruct one another, preferring rather to ask ourselves the sort of question which helps us to recognise the grounds for the leading. We try not to speak to or for ourselves, or to comment on something already said, though we accept that earlier ministry may well spark a contribution from another worshipper. It is remarkable how often something said by another may in fact provide a key to unlock our own thoughts. The experience also of a wholly silent Meeting can be a most moving and uplifting experience.

Seeking the Light through silence is a tradition which we in Britain treasure. We find it offers us a way to the Light while also giving us the opportunity to benefit from the contributions of other worshippers. Silence can of course have two faces: the silence of seeking, and the silence of emptiness, for example when members are engaged in private meditation, this leaves a void that can be felt. This discipline which we each exercise over our worship is something that is hard to share with casual visitors who occasionally treat us as a free pulpit for one of their personal concerns.

Meetings for Worship in Britain are normally unprogrammed, that is to say we have no leader or organised singing, reading or prayer. Though this follows the earliest practices of Quakers, today it is the minority form of worship among Friends worldwide. Most Quakers in other parts of the world include an address from a Pastor or some formal prayers or hymns as well as a period of silence. British Sunday Meetings usually last for one hour, though on occasion they may be lengthened or shortened if it seems right (Friends occasionally joke about how often the Spirit seems to prompt the ending on the hour or half hour).

Though we have no Pastors in Britain, we sometimes need to ask a Friend to give an introduction when there is a special Meeting for Worship on occasions such as a wedding or funeral, because these will attract many people who are not familiar with the practices of the Society, but though one person will introduce the Meeting and may well also signal when he or she feels it should end, they are not the leader but merely the chosen servant of the Meeting for that event.

Quaker approach to Religion

We have no separate priesthood nor do we rely on statements of belief to unite us, but this is not to say that we do not use passages from books or poems, including the Bible, which we may find helpful in our spiritual lives. One such, also found as Chapter 1 in Quaker Faith and Practice, is our "Advices and Queries". This booklet has a long history in the Society, filling the need for some more practical advice than simply the injunction to "live in the Light". As their name implies, they avoid the prescriptive form of the Ten Commandments, while helping us gently to examine our lives and actions as Jesus did in his summary of the Law. Quakerism attempts to retain the same spirit, while offering a different approach to religion. Mainstream Christianity is founded on certain specific beliefs about Jesus and the events in his life, while our approach is based rather on the implications of his teaching and how far we can live in its spirit. From this point of view, we may have more in common with the other main world religions than with traditional Christianity.

A Christian Church?

Quakerism has always avoided developing a detailed theology, because the Society was formed at a time when people could still remember the religious persecutions of the Reformation, in which both sides persecuted the other when in power. One of our earliest insights was that words divided people far more than they united them. This absence of a Creed or Statement of Belief from our spiritual life is one of the aspects which most worries other Christian groups. "Churches Together in Britain and Ireland" have produced special wording in its constitution to enable us to be members. This decision was not welcome to some Evangelical Churches, so it is useful for us to have a form of words which save us from getting enmeshed in complicated theological dialogues with members of these Churches. One such reply to the question, "Are you a Christian?" could be: "I try to follow the teachings of Jesus."

Though our origins are Christian, we differ from other Christian denominations in that we require no statements of belief nor do we attribute absolute authority to the words of any version of the Bible. We do not even require belief in the divinity of Jesus, or that mankind is essentially sinful. For us religion is about how we live, and we find that the Light not only illuminates our spiritual and everyday lives but can also be enjoyed in our experience of beauty in all its forms.

Though we try to be guided by Jesus' teaching, we do not

regard the gospel stories as being necessarily completely authentic; we try to test them with the insights of modern scholarship and the leadings of others through the ages up to the present. We believe that the Spirit, which is reflected in the life and teachings of Jesus of Nazareth, has spoken both before and after his life, and continues to inspire mankind today. But for such new inspirations to be trusted, we must examine them in the light of our own deepest experience.

Religion and Uncertainty

Our freedom from doctrinal orthodoxy brings us the problems, and opportunities, of uncertainty. As Karen Armstrong puts it in her "A History of God": "Like art, religion has been an attempt to find meaning and value in life, despite the sufferings that flesh is heir to. .... it is natural to humanity." Because of our Christian tradition, most people in this country think religion means having a belief in a Supreme Being who created the world and all that is in it and, in addition, promises a reward after death if one has meet the required criteria - usually involving a good life and adherence to certain doctrines. Most Quakers do not feel that there is any certain knowledge about existence after our lives, nor any evidence for the qualifications for entry into it. We are likely to assent to the proposition that if there is a purpose to human existence, then it is most likely to do with the expression of love in this life and so, regardless of whether it is rewarded after death or not, we try to live such lives.

We also differ from most other Protestant bodies in giving primacy to the leadings of the Spirit rather than treating the Bible as the absolute Word of God. While most Quakers recognise that parts of the Bible are truly inspired, we do not require assent to the doctrine of the "Atonement" (that Jesus was required to die for our sins) nor recognise the spiritual necessity or validity of Baptism, the Eucharist, Consecration or Ordination; we do not even require belief in the divinity of Jesus, though many Friends do so believe.

We also recognise that there are truths known in other religions which Christianity has not discovered. The teachings of the Buddha speak to many Quakers. We do not believe however that language, nor indeed the human brain, is capable of fully understanding or expressing spiritual matters.

Perhaps my experience with our late cat Sandy might help illustrate what I am trying to say. It seemed to me that for him I had only two functions: I was a tin-opener and a lap. He appeared to believe that I had also a relationship with doors, but was unclear how to activate it, however, when he sat on my lap and gazed into my eyes I felt that he had some recognition that I was a conscious being. A cat is a relatively advanced animal, nearer to me than I am to the most minimal deity that I can conceive. I believe that any human understanding of the divine (and the words in which it is expressed) will be at least as limited as Sandy's was of me.

Such doctrinal freedom does not seem to be shared by any other western denomination. The uncertainty resulting from our rejection of dogma has, as its other face, the freedom of belief and conscience. We gain guidance but are not compelled into conformity. We have for a long time had the clear understanding that religion is about how we should try to live our lives, not about the words we use to describe the divinity or our relationship with it. We do not demand success in this endeavour as a qualification for Membership of the Society (I for one would not be a Member if it did), but rather are looking for sincerity and integrity in our attempts to live "in the Light". We are of course not alone, having the support of loving friends both in our Meetings for Worship and in our daily lives. We can recognise our weaknesses but because we are not burdened with a fear of damnation, we can start each day anew, being mindful only of the need to rectify harmful things we may have done or said.

Sacraments

From the earliest days of Quakerism, we have regarded all days and places as equally holy. Early Quakers got into a lot of trouble for opening their shops on Sundays. Although we do now generally have our principal Meeting for Worship on Sundays, this is for convenience rather than as a matter of principle. We do not have any special celebration on Easter or Christmas nor even on Whitsunday - as might be expected for the day the Apostles are said to have received that same Spirit we recognise today. We do hold special Meetings for Worship to celebrate a marriage or partnership, but this is an act of celebration and witness (and is also recognised by the State). We regard the whole of life, indeed the whole of the world, as potentially sacramental. We recognise that we need reminders of this belief in our busy lives. Many of us try to make our meals meaningful with a short period of silent worship to give thanks for the food and fellowship, which we regard as sacramental, though in a different spirit from the formalised communions at other Churches. One of my Friends used to say she had no problems with treating all meals as sacramental, it was the washing-up that she found difficult.

Our belief in the sacramental nature of all life and hence in the absence of boundaries between the sacred and profane means that we do not consider our buildings as "consecrated", holy places which require a restricted access. We can use them for any purpose and often let them out to other organisations, though we try to ensure that the activities which take place are compatible with our general principles. Perhaps the key aspect of our belief in the sacramental nature of the world is our belief that human life in particular is sacred. This is the prime, though not the sole, factor underlying our rejection of war, as will be considered in the next section.

Rituals

In spite of what we often claim, Quakers do not lack rituals, though I think it is right to say that these are generally those which help us reinforce our fellowship (like shaking hands with our neighbours at the close of Meeting) rather than ones which might be thought to affect our spiritual condition. I remember when I was a new Member being constantly asked if I enjoyed the freedom of "having no ritual". I used to ask if they were joking. Quakers have lots of rituals, running from the use of formal phrases to standing and waiting silently until we are called by the Clerk in our Business Meetings. The big difference is that we do not attach a spiritual meaning to them.

LIVING

The Quaker Testimonies

Religion means little if it is not about how you try to live. Religion that is only about belief is mere superstition. All of our Testimonies, or guiding principles - to Truth, Justice, Simplicity, Equality and Peace, remain essentially unchanged from those which were developed by George Fox. They reflect our understanding of Jesus' teaching. Over the centuries, different issues have had primacy in Quaker life. In the seventeenth century, Truth was a major issue because of the requirement to swear oaths in Court, which Quakers refused both because that implied a double standard of truth and also because Jesus forbade it to his disciples. Though some might feel these "Testimonies" are substitutes for creeds and that one would not be welcome in the Society if, for example, one were not a pacifist, this is not so. These principles are more in the nature of headlines from which we start our search for the way forward, one which is right for us as individuals. In these, as in our other beliefs, we are not required to succeed, only to be trying to live in the Light.

Peace

Today one of the best-known features of Quakerism is our "Peace Testimony". It has gained this position not only because in the two World Wars our stand for conscientious objection led to a considerable influx of new members for whom non-violence was a primary concern, but also because of our continuing active objection to nuclear weapons and the arms trade. Our rejection of war, though intrinsic to Fox's understanding of the workings of the Spirit, gains much of its contemporary authority because it is the only one definitively stated in the seventeenth century. It is recorded in a pamphlet published by Friends in 1660 to explain our pacifism when Quakers were being blamed for an attempted coup against Charles II. The original wording reflects the concern about the use of force for political ends. When we rephrase it today, we lay more emphasis on the need for reconciliation and on alternatives to violence. However, we still hold that it is neither true to the Light in us, nor does it respect the Light in the other, to kill, or even to harm or deceive another person.

It might also be appropriate to mention here the action taken by Quakers around the country to demonstrate both their opposition to the attacks of September 11th 2001, and subsequently to those by our government on Afghanistan and Iraq. Our silent public vigils clearly reflected a widely-held concern and provided a necessary peaceful focus for those who wanted this view to be seen (including members of the Armed Forces). I particularly remember the senior officer who spent a long time reading our leaflet and discussing it with his wife before coming to me and saying that he wished us well, though if we were successful he would lose his job. His wife added that she would be praying for us.

Truth

Speaking Truth at all times is important, and is also very challenging since the commitment implies that we should at all times be careful how we use words, not just when we are on oath. Everyone now has the right to "affirm" in Court, but since the permitted form of words really only omits the use of the word "God", it still implies two standards of truth. I once agreed to affirm in Court, but afterwards wished I had insisted on using no form of words, but to accept that I would be committing perjury if I said things which were not true.

Equality & Justice

Our belief in Equality and Justice, between genders, races and ages, has inspired us from the beginning to remove barriers that restricted women's activities, to be innovators in the education of children and to inspire the campaign against slavery. Imprisonment, which thousands of early Quakers endured for their beliefs, has made the Society very conscious of the criminal justice system and many Friends have worked, and still work, at a variety of levels, to improve it. We are now facing new challenges with the widespread discrimination against those seeking asylum and the growth of new, insidious, forms of slavery in this country.

Our early concern for **Simplicity**, which initially led us to adopt distinctive clothes (now seen only on porridge oats' cartons) leads us today to support environmental sustainability and to adopt a lifestyle that minimises waste and heavy consumption. This concern will also help us to face the challenges of global warming.

Evil and Suffering

Most Christians, and indeed most people in this country, find difficulty in reconciling the idea of a "loving" God with the world they see around them. While Quakers feel that the Spirit that can inspire anyone, leads us towards love, few of us believe that the Spirit influences or controls the natural processes of the world. We do not believe that natural disasters, such as earthquakes, volcanoes, tsunamis and plagues, are provided for a purpose and adapted to protect or test the good and punish the wicked. The way we see the Spirit operating is by "the promptings of love and truth in our hearts" (1.02.1). It prompts us when we listen, but it does not command - and nor does it force us to listen. Quakers are not prone to ask themselves after a natural disaster "How could a loving God allow this?" Such events, however, are likely to inspire us to respond individually with compassion and aid. Other events however, such as floods, droughts and landslips, often have a human cause which we can help to mitigate. Our testimonies to equality and simplicity come to mind.

Though we believe that there is a divine spark in everyone, there are plenty of pressures which can lead anyone to act in selfish or even cruel ways. Our belief in the universality of the Light does not prevent us from recognising evil in people nor their blindness to the Light, nor does it prevent us from supporting preventive measures. We usually however question the value of punishment, looking rather for a response which would lead to reform. One advantage of our beliefs and form of worship is that it helps us to resist external pressures and to listen to what our hearts are trying to say and overcome our own vengeful thoughts.

Other Faiths

Many years ago I heard a Friend describe the tapestry of world religions as an enormous stained glass window in which we are all fragments of glass of different colours and sizes but, because we can have no idea of the whole picture, we cannot say that our size, shape or colour is any better or worse than another's. Our responsibility is to transmit the Light as honestly and clearly as possible. We recognised from the earliest years of the Society that there can be no single way to the Light. There are many paths to the Truth or the Divine and, while our roots are in Christianity, we do not believe that all other Faiths are wrong or misguided. Our problems tend to be with those which hold to absolute and exclusive beliefs. Our relations with Christian Churches therefore tend to be with those in the mainstream rather than with the more evangelical ones, who often regard us as heretical because of our attitude to the Bible. Our approach to other Faiths is open-minded and we take all opportunities to forge bonds with them. We see glimmerings of the Light not only in the Bible but also in the Koran and in other religious writings.

We always need, particularly in our contacts with the non-Christian religions, to emphasise that we are a Spirit-led body and that, though we developed from Christianity, we do not require a belief in the divine nature of Jesus nor in the Trinity, which are the main stumbling blocks for others. We also explain that we seek for an awareness of the Light and an intention to try to lead our lives in accordance with its leadings. This is reflected by the Standing Advisory Council for Religious Education in Devon, where we are grouped with Buddhists, Hindus, Humanists, Jews and Muslims as an "Other".

Most non-Christian Faiths, other than Islam, do not have mandatory doctrines, but it seems that none of the major Faith groupings have anything comparable to the extensive Anglican and Catholic Creeds or the Statements of Belief of some Dissenting Churches. Islam and Judaism have prescribed practices and extensive doctrinal teachings. Hinduism, Daoism and Buddhism also have extensive teachings, and in some the authority of teachers is very strictly enforced. However, all seem to have avoided the particular requirement of encapsulating their teachings in the form of lengthy statements mandatory on their membership that is typical of many branches of Christianity.

The Arts and Sciences

Early Quakers often rejected music and beauty in all their forms as distractions, perhaps not surprisingly in a Puritan age. Though this is no longer the case, we sometimes still bear the reputation of being killjoys. Early Friends lived at a time in which most Puritans saw pleasure as a distraction from the grim business of striving for salvation, even to the extent of smashing their musical instruments. Nowadays, we believe that it is right to rejoice in the beauties and pleasures of the world and believe that the joy we feel is the Light in us responding. Though few early Friends became known as painters or musicians, more recently we have had a few poets and even some actors, notably Paul Eddington and Judi Dench. There is also the remarkable "Quaker Tapestry" showing the history of the Society, embroidered by a large number of Friends, with some 70 panels on display in Kendal in the summer and in different Cathedrals in winter.

Early Friends were very active in the beginnings of the Industrial Revolution, both scientifically and as entrepreneurs, partly because, in common with members of the Catholic and Nonconformist Churches, they were not allowed to attend Oxford or Cambridge, which were then the only English universities. This restriction debarred them from the "learned" professions of Law and Teaching which were, up to the late nineteenth century, entirely the province of Anglicans.

Sciences, other than mathematics, were not taught even in these universities at this time and so the bright Nonconformist children studied science in the workplace. Quakers went into industry and played a very significant part in the developing studies of the natural sciences, though with a strong pacifist bias. They were at the forefront in practical matters such as the development of iron smelting at Coalbrookdale (although the Darbys ceased manufacture once the primary use for iron became weapons and armour plating). Others found different trades, for example: clothing (Clarks and Morland), pharmaceuticals (Allen & Hanbury), chocolate (Cadbury, Fry and Rowntree) and banking (Lloyds and Barclays) to name only a few.

However, with the opening of the universities to Dissenters from the middle of the nineteenth century, Quakers largely ceased to be business men and moved instead into the professions, principally teaching and social work of various kinds. The research tradition, however, has continued with particular success in physiology with Francis Dalton's discovery of colour-blindness through to astronomy, with Arthur Eddington's test for the theory of Relativity and with, in the later twentieth century, Jocelyn Burnell's discovery of the first pulsar.

Personal Morality

Not all the problems which we face are directly answered by the appropriate Testimony. To take gambling as an example, Quakers generally avoid not only straightforward gambling but also lotteries and raffles. Our objections to these activities spring from a variety of roots. We are very concerned about compulsive and habitual gambling and the distress and privation it can bring upon the family. We also object because it treats money not as the reward for value given but as something not earned, and in the case of the National Lottery, a snare offering chances of a big prize where the likelihood of anyone actually getting one are vanishingly small. Local charity lotteries are slightly different. I have bought tickets for such lotteries from time to time. Once to my embarrassment I won first prize - a fortnight's holiday in Florida for two. I tried to give the prize back, but they would not take it, saying that they had been offered the flight and accommodation free, so they would just have to find another recipient. I accepted, and had a most interesting and informative visit meeting Americans in the aftermath of the first Gulf War.

Alcohol is also a sensitive issue with Friends. Many of us are quite easy with alcohol in moderation but, like the Methodists, we do not normally allow alcohol on our Meeting House premises. As a Society we are concerned about alcoholism and are ready to make our premises available to Alcoholics Anonymous, but while some of us remain total abstainers (and most will drink nothing before driving) others feel that an example of moderation is at least as valuable as total abstinence. Here again I must admit to being a tempter. My wife and I reached our 40th wedding anniversary on the same day as another couple in the Meeting, and to enable us to celebrate together with Friends, our local prohibition on alcohol in the building was temporarily suspended.

Our personal sexual morality is not based on Biblical teaching but on the principle that we should not do anything that causes - or would have caused if it became known - any distress or unhappiness. This does not mean that we reject those who stray, but hope they will find a resolution satisfactory to all parties. We have no doctrinal problems with homosexuality. Most Meetings welcome and support same-sex partnerships and even in those Meetings which do not wish to recognise them formally, there will be no sense of rejection. In essence our personal, as well as our collective morality is based on Jesus' teaching to treat our neighbour as we would hope to be treated ourselves.

THE SOCIETY

The Structure of Quakerism

Our concept of "the priesthood of all believers" springs directly from our understanding of the universality of the Inward Light. This of course puts us in a slightly different position from members of other Christian churches. With no belief in the sacrament of Ordination, we all share responsibility for the worship and spiritual life of the Meeting. Of course we do delegate particular responsibilities to individuals, but these appointments are always only for a limited period. We do not want to create an elite of "virtual priests" and still less an underclass of permanent followers. The two main functions of a "priesthood" are fostering the learning and understanding within the group and the pastoral care of its members. Traditionally the Society has carried out these two separate functions by appointing "Elders" and "Overseers" for limited terms and though some Meetings share these forms of service among all the Members, there are always some duties which need to be allocated rather than shared.

One of the most remarkable achievements of the two principal founders of Quakerism, George Fox and Margaret Fell, was the creation of a structure which has enabled a Society, not bound by doctrine and with no paid priesthood, to last for over 350 years. Almost all the other radical groups which arose at the time of the Reformation have vanished or withered away to tiny remnants. The structure which Fox and Fell devised centers worship under the care of the Local Meeting, but puts administration and membership under an Area Meeting, a grouping of a number of Local Meetings (formerly referred to as a "Monthly Meeting"). This enables local initiatives or problems to be tested by a larger body. If a major change is proposed or one that would affect the whole Society, the matter will be referred to the Meeting for Sufferings, so-called because its first task was to relieve distress during the seventeenth century persecutions. Today together with the Trustees it forms the central deliberative body between sessions of the "Yearly Meeting" which is our "AGM" open to all British Quakers and is the ultimate authority for Friends in this country.

The pattern of having a single Yearly Meeting for England, Scotland and Wales (Ireland has its own Yearly Meeting) is repeated over the world, though with Yearly Meetings in the USA based more often on a single State rather than nation-wide. The one exception to this pattern of a hierarchy of geographically-based Meetings is the organisation for younger adults - the "Young Friends General Meeting". Since people between the ages of 18 and their early thirties are often very mobile, their decision to form a group which was not geographical has enabled them to play a much fuller part in the life of the Society as a whole, enabling them to speak, and be heard, as a group.

One development that was perhaps not foreseen in the seventeenth century was the growing involvement of the Society in a number of continuing concerns and campaigns such as peacemaking, disarmament, human rights, restorative justice, state education, homelessness etc. We have found it best to administer these projects with a paid staff. Supervision and management of this staff and their Committees, together with the supervision of their budgets, we now delegate to Trustees, a new small body which is answerable to and appointed by the Yearly Meeting. We have set up various functional Committees to be responsible for setting priorities and allocating resources to best effect under the budgetary control and supervision of the Trustees. The difficult decisions that this entails can cause great pain when we must allocate limited resources between different pressing needs, but we try always to ensure that they are taken after careful exercise of spiritual discernment and fully express the "sense of the Meeting". Working in parallel with the Trustees is the representative Meeting for Sufferings. This body is also answerable to the Yearly Meeting and is now primarily responsible for discerning how to focus the spiritual leadings of the Society.

Originally, in an age when travel and communication were difficult, George Fox and Margaret Fell set up General Meetings to act as an intermediary body between the Area and the Yearly Meeting. Nowadays we use them as gatherings for instruction and discussion, though in some areas they have been abandoned with the learning function provided at a more local level. In addition, though not as part of our decision-making structure, is the Friends World Committee for Consultation. This meets every three years to share experience and concerns; it brings Friends together who see Jesus as the only Son of God with those who see him as a great teacher, and those who worship in Silent Meetings with those from Meetings with appointed Pastors. Though these discussions are often difficult, they enable us to recognise our essential unity in the Light.

Quakerism and Children

There is an intrinsic problem with an experiential religion which is the question of teaching in particular the sharing of our insights with our young children. For those not yet in their teens we use the parables and stories of Jesus' teaching ministry, not to emphasise his divinity but rather as hints about how we should try to live our own lives. I believe we should try not to focus too much on attractive stories from our Quaker past, because ours is a religion for today. We should try rather to convey our beliefs by the way we approach the issues of the day. We can also show our belief that the Light is available to all, by showing our respect for the insights of the young. This can indeed be very successful with adolescents and young adults, but with the very young ones we perhaps do best by sharing our own enthusiasms, knowledge and our approach to contemporary problems with them and by listening to what they say. If we shy away from much traditional Bible teaching, we need to ask ourselves whether we put enough in its place.

Hierarchy - and how to avoid it

We have a hierarchy of Meetings, but not of people. Whereas in other organisations, someone can be appointed to the highest office and then may hold it to retirement, in our Society everyone taking up a responsible post is appointed for a three-year term with a possible extension for a second term, but no more. We do occasionally make exceptions for positions which require special skills, such as treasurers, but we keep these to a minimum. This practice can demand much more of each ordinary member than would be the case in another Church, but it also spreads experience more widely and frees us from a lifetime commitment to any one task. Such a system depends to a very large extent on the selection process. This is done by a series of nomination committees whose own membership is chosen by others, not party to the appointments to be made.

Decision making

Our "Meetings for Worship for Church Affairs" (our Business Meetings) are held as a prayerful search for the right way forward. We make our decisions not by deciding by majority vote but by considering the issue until we have found "the sense of the Meeting" and can agree on the way forward. This is not "consensus", which we take to be a sort of lowest common denominator, but rather the highest common factor, the outcome that feels right to all when we hold it in the Light. We do not expect to be guided to, say, choose one colour rather than another for painting our Meeting Room, but we trust that both the way we reach a decision and that the answer we find feel to have been led by the Spirit.

This decision-making method, which is not divisive if properly carried out, is one of the most unusual features of Quakerism. It puts a particular responsibility on the Clerk, who is the servant of the Meeting, rather than a controlling "Chairman". In these Meetings, the Clerk proposes the Agenda, but does not speak on any item other than to introduce the matter or to call on people who wish to contribute until he or she feels (or discerns) that the Meeting is moving towards a decision. The Clerk will then draft a Minute recording what feels like the decision and reads it to the Meeting. If it is acceptable to all, then that is the decision. If there are further comments which would amend the decision, the Clerk may redraft the minute and will continue to do so until all feel satisfied that the right way forward has been found.

When we have a complex issue to decide, we sometimes separate the consideration into two distinct stages: first, to try to understand and agree on the facts and issues which are relevant, then, in the second stage, to try worshipfully to find the right answer. On occasion it may be that no unity is found and in such a case the matter will be deferred to allow time for further consideration. Such a method is not quick, but it does have the practical consequence that once agreed, decisions can be quickly and efficiently carried out without hidden resistance. It requires qualities in the Clerk that are not needed by a conventional Chair. I experienced a remarkable example of such a meeting when there was a proposal to rebuild a Meeting House. An Architect had produced plans which the Building Committee endorsed and recommended to a Meeting for Church Affairs attended by about 200 Friends. One Friend realised that the design would be most unwelcoming for strangers and spoke out. Even though he was only supported by one or two other Friends, the Clerk decided to defer a decision until alternative proposals could be considered. When it met again, the Meeting accepted a totally new proposal, not in fact one put forward by the original objector, (nor the Architect!) but one which has since won universal admiration.

Our Tools

Although we regard the Bible as a collection of writings, some of which are inspired, we do not take it as authoritative for individual actions today, nor do we believe that revelation ceased with the fourth century of the Christian Era. We believe that the Spirit continues to speak to those of any Faith who will listen, accepting that all will interpret insights they receive within the framework of their own individual tradition.

This diversity is reflected in our anthology of Quaker thought, "Quaker Faith & Practice". This great collection of writings includes passages covering the whole experience of the Society. We revise it about every generation and drop those passages which no longer seem relevant and add (or recover) others for which the time feels right. I find it a most inspiring book, though curiously it was not its inspirational passages that led me to apply for membership. At the time I discovered the Society, I was rewriting my Department's office manual and the contrast between what I was doing and the enabling and sensitive approach of the administrative sections of "Church Government" (as it was then called) made me sure that Quakers were a body to which I needed to belong.

The opening chapter of Quaker Faith and Practice, "Advices & Queries" were originally a means of encouraging uniformity of practice among early Friends. We have found it a useful format to modify regularly to match the changes in society. We also use it today as a source of occasional readings in our Meetings for Worship. It is available as a separate pocket book and it, together with the complete Quaker Faith & Practice and the Bible, will be found on the table at all our Meetings. Most Meetings will also have libraries containing writings of many faiths, though primarily Christian. Even those small Meetings which do not have their own premises will have collections in the homes of their Members. We are a very literate Society, a fact which may tend to work against our wider appeal.

Quakerism Today

We are still "Seekers", people who share a belief that being required to assent to fixed beliefs shackles the Spirit. This approach is diametrically opposed to all fundamentalist views of religion, but increasingly resonates with many who reject simplistic and dogmatic teaching.

We believe that the stresses which are becoming apparent over the world are made more dangerous if the principles of the opposed groups do not permit understanding of the other's point of view. There is also a second danger which, though insidious, is not less threatening. There is in this country, I believe, a haziness of mind, a half-heartedness and general undervaluing of the place of thought in religion. This is not to argue for set beliefs, but to point the need to become more aware of the importance which religious, ethical and moral thinking ought to play even in the most mundane and practical matters. We need to provide opportunities for the Light to shine. This should not be the case in Quaker business only, but could become the practice in all situations where it is more important to reach a right decision than to win an argument.

Because the Quaker understanding of religion is based on personal experience and understanding of the spiritual power of the Light, rather than on doctrines taught by others, it is difficult to explain to people brought up in a secular environment. It however enables us to link religion to the principles of love, truth and beauty, rather than to history. It can also inspire those who feel hampered in their spiritual growth by the need to conform to another's view of Truth. Consequently, not being constrained by the need to conform to dogma and yet being believers in a divine Power accessible to all, helps Quakers to speak to other Faiths without feeling a need to challenge their beliefs. In fact there are a number of Friends who take part in Buddhist worship, as well as those who also attend local Church services.

I believe I share with all 21st century Friends the conviction that it is more important that world faiths build bridges between one another rather than focusing on conversion. We are living in very dangerous times, not only from terrorism and the probable effects of global warming and pollution but also from the injustices of capitalism and the sterilities of religious fundamentalism. Now is a time for all people who are concerned primarily about truth, simplicity, justice, equality and peace to unite to speak honestly and openly with one another. We will never all share the same beliefs, indeed it is better that we are not all identical, but we need to have a level on which we can meet. Dogma is our enemy and in resisting dogma, it is vital to have a clear understanding of the basis of Quakerism. All we need is the Light, if only we can learn to recognise it.

"Our life is love, and peace, and tenderness; and bearing one with another, and forgiving one another, and not laying accusations one against another; but praying one for another, and helping one another up with a tender hand."

Isaac Penington, 1667 (QF&P 10.01)

Afterword

This is a very brief and personal introduction to 21st century Quakerism and how it developed. It is written in the hope that understanding more about the Society will enable you to get more out of any Meetings for Worship you may attend. Not having the formal "teaching ministry" of other Churches, puts an obligation onto each of us to be responsible for our own learning - and of course to help one another. The books suggested on the following pages will give you a variety of views. Quakerism is not a soft option, but neither does it require you to assent to statements with which you do not feel in agreement. To take membership seriously means that you must take responsibility for your own spiritual development, which can offer spiritual riches which will repay your efforts many times over. Membership becomes appropriate when you feel you are comfortable with the Quaker way, and feel you want to be known as a member of the Religious Society of Friends. Reluctance to take up membership because of a feeling of "unworthiness" shows a mistaken view of Quakerism. If we have a reputation as "good", it is possibly because we try to express our beliefs in action rather than in words.

If you decide that you would like to join the Society, a full description of how to do it can be found in QF&P Chapter 11 (detail in 11.07). The procedure is designed to provide a setting in which you can share your spiritual journey with Friends who have trodden the same path before you.

Notes on suggested Books:

Rex Ambler Truth of the Heart
An anthology of George Fox's writings selected and translated for the modern reader.

Sydney Bailey,   Peace is a Process
This gives a full history of Quaker peace work, focusing on his own experience up to the 1970s. It does not examine other areas of Quaker work or concerns. It does not deal with more recent developments such as work on reconciliation and training for avoidance of conflict (AVP).

Michael Birkel   Silence & Witness
This is possibly the best survey of Quaker history and the development of Quaker thought in the early years of the Society. Ideal for those who are curious about our beginnings.

Harvey Gilman   A Light that is Shining
The definitive introduction to Quakerism which is very useful for the beginner, though recent changes in the administration of the Society have made some passages obsolete.

George Gorman The Amazing Fact of Quaker Worship
This is an excellent introduction to the Meeting for Worship and our discipline. It does not deal with our administrative structure and so does not need updating.

Thomas Kelly   A Testament of Devotion
A meditation on the spiritual life which has become a Christian classic far beyond the confines of the Society. Its five sections address the Light within, holy obedience, community, social concern and the simplification of life.

Rosemary Moore The Light in their Consciences

A history of the early years with particularly useful discussions on the principal characters and the development of the Society before 1666

Barry Morley   Beyond Consensus

A practical American account of the spirit behind our decision-making process. Very readable and full of sound practical advice.

John Punshon   Portrait in Grey

A "warts and all" portrait with a light touch and a happy turn of phrase - and an excellent explanation of why "Puritanism" is not a dirty word. A history book with a difference.

John Punshon   Encounter with Silence

This account of the transformation of an individual life into the freedom and joy of one totally obedient to the leadings of the Spirit will inspire and guide everyone who wants to explore the Quaker route to spiritual development.

Philip Rack   Quakerism in the 21st Century

This gives more detail about the Society and its history in a most accessible manner. It also addresses some of the questions with which Quakers are currently wrestling. Well worth reading.

Michael Sheeran Beyond Majority Rule

The work of a Jesuit scholar who was fascinated by our method of trying to discover the right solution. It is probably the best work on this important aspect of the Society and, in spite of being scholarly, is a gripping read.

Alex Wildwood   A faith to call our own

This links contemporary Quakerism to new spirituality in a world that has ever increasing (scientific) knowledge but less wisdom. It records his experience of his inner spiritual journey sharing his story with many of the New Age movements.

Quaker Faith and Practice

An anthology of Quaker writings which is updated about every twenty years. It is an inspired work, combining guidelines to the organisation of the Society with passages relevant to contemporary issues. This is the central work of reference for all British, and most European Quakers.

And finally

Any booklet in the series **"Twelve Quakers and ...."** Each one contains the reflections of the group on one of the following issues: Jesus, Simplicity, Evil, Pacifism, Worship, God and (finally) Equality.

All the above can be obtained from:
The Quaker Bookshop   (Tel: 020 7663 1030)
173 Euston Rd
LONDON NW1 2BJ